John Wesley Powell

Soldier Explorer Scientist

John Wesley Powell

Soldier Explorer Scientist

A NOW YOU KNOW BIO

Jean Thor Cook

Filter Press, LLC
Palmer Lake, Colorado

This book is dedicated to my family
who are strong in spirit,
share a love of adventure,
and roll up their sleeves to get a job done.

To
Annika, Kastine, Annalise, Kris, Nathaniel, Tom,
Audrey, Ben, Kara, Katie,
Katie Marie, Jon, Rob, Jill, Pam, Terry, Jodi, Siri,
Ralph, and Alan

ISBN-13: 978-0-86541-080-0
Library of Congress Control Number: 2006933693

Maps by Janice Niblack, pages 32-33, 38.
Illustration by David W. Jones, pages 11, 21, 26.

Filter Press, LLC, P.O. Box 95, Palmer Lake, Colorado
www.filterpressbooks.com

Printed in the United States of America

Contents

"The glories of the beauties of form, color, and sound unite in the Grand Canyon ...It has infinite variety, and no part is ever duplicated. Its colors, though many and complex at any instant, change with the ascending and declining sun; lights and shadows appear and vanish with the passing clouds, and the changing season mark their passage in changing colors."

J. W. Powell

The Exploration of the Colorado River and Its Canyons, 1875

1 Young Scientist

Even when he was nine years old, red-headed John Wesley Powell couldn't wait to explore nature. Shy and intelligent, "Wes" was born in 1834 in Mount Morris, New York. Now he lived in Jackson, Ohio. In time, his curiosity about nature led him on a path to fame. He became one of America's outstanding explorers and scientists.

Neither of Wes's parents—Joseph or Mary Powell—took their son to explore nature. Poor **immigrants** who **emigrated** from Great Britain, their days were jam-packed with work. They wanted to buy lots of land, sell it for more than they paid for it, and stop being poor.

Joseph had two jobs: tailor and Methodist minister. He sewed clothes for the folks in Jackson and for his family. When he wasn't sewing, he rode his horse

John Wesley Powell's parents, Mary and Joseph Powell, came to America from Great Britain. Mary was born in England. Joseph (probably born 1805) was of Welsh heritage. The Welsh are noted for their singing. Mary and Joseph were devout Methodists.

through the Ohio countryside preaching sermons. He liked preaching sermons more than sewing clothes.

Mary took good care of their eight children. She washed clothes, grew food in huge gardens, and cooked meals. Busy as she was, she made time to teach all eight of her children to read. At night, she played the piano and taught them to sing.

So who did take Wes into the out-of-doors to observe nature? Who started him on the road to becoming one of America's famous explorers and scientists?

It was old George Crookham, a friend of the Powell family. Crookham liked taking Wes on wagon rides to collect **specimens** and **artifacts** for his **natural history museum**. Now that Crookham's sixteen children were grown, Wes was company for the old man.

George Crookham was smart. He had a library of books at a time when few people knew how to read. He read and spoke Latin. Once, he surprised folks by reading a newspaper upside down. Best of all, he was a walking storehouse of knowledge on many subjects, especially nature.

On Crookham's farm was a log building. Crookham used one side of the building as a school where adults learned to read. The other side held a natural history museum. In the museum were specimens such as snake skins, plants, unusual rocks, Native American arrowheads, and mounted birds and animals. Everything in the museum fascinated Wes.

Because Crookham knew a lot about many subjects, folks often came to him for information. The people in Jackson agreed Crookham was a smart man, but they didn't always like what he said. Crookham was an **abolitionist**. So were the Powells. Abolitionists worked to abolish slavery. They helped slaves escape to the North to freedom. This angered the people who wanted slavery. They wanted to keep slaves as their personal property. After all, it was the slaves who did the backbreaking farmwork and housework. And hadn't the slave owners paid a lot of money for them?

Joseph Powell gave fiery sermons on the evils of slavery. Hatreds smoldered, then ignited. Standing up for abolishing slavery was risky business. It was a time when people threw rocks at folks who disagreed with them. The Powells worried about Wes. Would the boys at school throw rocks at him? At nine years of age, Wes was good with his fists and not one to back down, but he was no match for a mob of bullies.

Some children did throw rocks at Wes. He came home with a bloody face and bruised body. Mary Powell sent for George Crookham. Crookham invited Wes to live with him. He would protect and teach Wes. Instead of being in the local

Courtesy Jackson County Supervisors. Jackson, Ohio. Susan Blanton, artist.

George Crookham, a family friend, had a great influence in Wes's love for geology and nature.

schoolhouse with a poorly educated teacher, he'd be with George Crookham. Wes was delighted.

Crookham was an excellent teacher. He took Wes into the countryside and taught him about the sciences that were part of **natural history**. Wes learned **ethnology, chemistry, biology,** and **geology.** Crookham's friend William Mather sometimes rode with them. Mather taught Wes **surveying** and showed him local geological formations. Wes also read books on **archaeology** and history from Crookham's library.

As they rode on field trips in Crookham's wagon or walked through the countryside, Crookham talked and taught. He told Wes what he knew of the environment that surrounded them. Together, they listened for bird songs. They looked at the trees and plants, and rocks and soil.

They opened mounds left behind by Native Americans to find out what they held. Wes dug **fossils** out of rocks. He helped collect bags of specimens to bring to Crookham's museum. At the museum, Wes dissected birds and animals to see what they ate. He examined **minerals**, salts, and coal and whatever else he found. By lamplight, Wes wrote down his findings in notebooks. He was learning to be a **curator**.

In Ohio, as in much of the United States, the arguments over slavery grew bitter. As the bitterness grew, the pro-slavery folks in Jackson became suspicious of Crookham. They had reason to be. One day, Wes saw Crookham put a mysterious bag into the wagon. Then, with Wes beside him, he drove to a river cave. Out of the cave came three runaway slaves. The bag contained food and clothing. Crookham told Wes that he was part of the **underground railroad** that helped slaves secretly travel north to freedom.

During this time, life became scary for Crookham and the Powell family. **Vandals** rode into Crookham's farmyard. They burned the school and museum to the ground. Crookham wept. His life's work was destroyed. More acts of hatred came. Someone cut off the mane and tail from the Powell's horse. Joseph Powell was attacked by people throwing stones.

Joseph and Mary Powell decided it was time to leave Ohio. The family packed their belongings into two wagons and traveled north to Wisconsin. They left Mary's beloved piano behind. There simply was no room in either of the wagons for it. Before they left, friends came to say good-bye. Some camped with them the first night.

Wes, now twelve years old, said a sad good-bye to George Crookham. That was the last time he saw the kind, smart old man who loved nature. Crookham died soon after. But his memory lived on. He influenced John Wesley Powell all his life.

After a month on dusty, rutted roads in creaking wagons, the Powell family of ten arrived in Wisconsin and bought a farm.

It was on that Wisconsin farm that Wes's dreams and his father's plans clashed.

2 Fighting Slavery

In 1846, the Powell wagons came to a halt in the southeast corner of Wisconsin. Joseph immediately bought a farm in Walworth County. It was near a town later called South Grove.

Once there, Joseph gave Wes some bad news. Wes wasn't going to school to study nature and learn science. Instead, the twelve-year-old boy was going to manage the family farm and support all ten members of the Powell family.

Then Joseph got on his horse and left home to be a full-time preacher.

Wes must have been startled because he knew nothing about farming. But then, neither did Joseph. In 1846, many boys quit school at a young age to farm. Without modern machinery, parents needed many hands to help raise crops and take care of animals.

⟨◆⟩

What was different here was that most boys had their fathers working beside them. As they worked together, the fathers taught their sons how to farm.

Amazingly, Wes and his brothers learned how to farm on their own. They asked questions. Then they plowed, planted, harvested, and sold wheat.

During this time, none of the money earned was Wes's. It all went to support the Powell family.

In 1850, after the harvest, Wes insisted his father come home. Wes was sixteen years old and done with farming. That's all there was to it. It was time for him to go to school. He aimed to earn a college degree in science.

Wes walked twenty miles to the nearest school in Janesville, Wisconsin. The teacher was a disappointment. Mary Powell understood her son's frustration with the poor education he was receiving. She had an idea. She encouraged Wes to become a teacher.

In 1852, Wes took books on grammar, mathematics, and **geography** to the Powell family attic. He crammed for six weeks, then walked thirty miles over frozen roads to his first job in Jefferson County, Wisconsin. His students—young and old—liked their teenage teacher. They especially liked his evening classes in geography. When Wes taught, he used catchy rhymes to help students remember the names of the states and their capitals. And he led his students in rousing songs such as "Uncle Sam's Farm." The song had a popular message. It said Uncle Sam was wealthy enough to give everyone a farm.

Mary and Joseph Powell sold their Wisconsin farm and moved to Illinois. Here they bought and sold land. Their plan to earn money by buying and selling at a profit paid off. In time, they had a comfortable living. They weren't rich, but they weren't poor. They ended up building a home in Wheaton, where there was a new college named Illinois Institute. It was renamed Wheaton College in 1860. Several of the Powell children attended this local college.

Wes attended three colleges trying to earn a science degree. One of them was Illinois Institute. The other two were Illinois College in Jacksonville and Oberlin in Ohio. It was a time of frustration for him. Illinois College offered science courses, but he couldn't afford the tuition. Oberlin and Illinois Institute didn't offer the classes he needed for a science major. Wes was serious about earning a college degree in science, but he never did.

During this time, Joseph tried desperately to persuade Wes to become a minister. Didn't Wes remember that he'd been named for the famous evangelist John Wesley, who founded the Methodist church? Being a minister wasn't Wes's plan. He wanted a life in science, so he seesawed back and forth between teaching, being a principal, and taking whatever science classes he could find.

Then Wes found another way to learn science. He went into the out-of-doors. He walked in America's forests and rowed on its rivers. There was no reason why he couldn't study nature and collect specimens on his own. He especially liked to collect **mollusk** shells, both freshwater and ancient saltwater fossils.

In 1855, when he was twenty-one, Wes walked from St. Paul, Minnesota, to Detroit, Michigan. In Detroit, he met his future wife, Emma Dean. She was full of spunk. Without a

Mollusk shells

steady income to provide a home, Wes couldn't marry Emma. She was willing to wait.

Wes rowed the entire length of the mighty Mississippi River in 1856. He traveled over 1,000 miles from St. Paul, Minnesota, to New Orleans, Louisiana.

Wes's life was unsettled, and so was America's.

‹◆›

Emma Dean Powell followed her husband to battlefields throughout the Civil War. This was typical of officers' wives. Emma took care of Major Powell after he was wounded. She was a tiny woman with a strong spirit of adventure.

John Wesley Powell, age 29, in his Civil War uniform. His right sleeve is empty because his forearm was amputated after he was shot during the Battle of Shiloh.

Arguments about slavery had erupted into the Civil War. The Southern Confederate army battled against the Northern Union army. Sad-eyed President Abraham Lincoln told the Confederates to free their slaves. And he told them something else they didn't want to hear. He said the United States government was the boss. It had the power to make decisions when it came to what was good for all its citizens.

The Southerners disagreed and war followed. More than 600,000 American lives were lost before the war ended.

Wes left his job as a school principal and joined the Union army in 1861, five days after President Lincoln called for volunteers. The army records listed him as five-feet-six inches tall, with gray eyes and auburn hair.

Know More!

Wes was named for John Wesley (1703-1791), a famous English preacher. It was Wesley who began the Methodist church. He preached that each person was a child of God. He was against slavery and for bringing a better life to the poor. He traveled 5,000 miles a year, mostly on horseback, to give his sermons. Sometimes he preached five sermons in one day.

Were you named after someone special? If so, who was it? f not, do you wish you were? If you could change your name, what name would you choose? Why?

He bought books on military engineering. From those books, he learned how to build defenses to protect the Union soldiers during battle.

During the fall of 1861, Brigadier General Ulysses S. Grant, commander of the Union army, came to see what Wes had built. Impressed, he asked Wes to become one of his officers.

General Ulysses S. Grant, commander of the Union army.

But Grant didn't want Wes to build defenses. Instead Grant made Wes an **artillery** commander.

Wes's younger brother Walter left teaching to join the Union army, too. He served under Wes's command.

That same year, Wes married Emma. Like many officers' wives, she followed her husband from one battleground to another. She was with him when he needed her at Shiloh.

In the terrible battle at Shiloh, bugles sounded their alert. Drums rolled. Men on both sides yelled their battle cries. Bayonets clashed, stabbing and killing. Horses screamed in pain as they were shot out from under officers. Men fought, and men ran for cover. The smoke of gunfire hung heavy between the trees. Strangely, when there was a moment of quiet, the sweet singing of birds could be heard.

The Battle of Shiloh changed Wes's life forever. On April 6, 1862, he raised his right hand to signal his gunners to stand clear. As he did, a musket ball shattered his arm. The lower part of his right arm was a bloody mess of broken bone and torn flesh. His brother Walter stopped the blood from flowing by applying a **tourniquet**. He helped Wes to a tree where there was shade. Two days later, the doctors amputated his arm below the elbow to save Wes's life. Emma went to the hospital to nurse her injured husband.

Despite being an amputee, Wes stayed in the army until 1865 and kept fighting until he knew the war

April 6, 1862. Twenty thousand men were wounded or killed in one day in the Civil War battle at Shiloh, Tennessee. Wes Powell was gravely wounded in the battle.

Know More!

During the battle at Shiloh, Union soldier Major Powell lost his right arm and Confederate officer Colonel Charles E. Hooker lost his left. After the Civil War, the men became friends and shared pairs of gloves. Major Powell used the left hand glove and Colonel Hooker the right.

was ending. He was often sick. The injured arm never stopped hurting. At one point, he weighed only 110 pounds.

During the war, Wes earned the rank of major. After that, he preferred to be called Major Powell. And that's what we'll call him from now on.

As the war ended, Major Powell had worrisome questions.

Where was Walter? Major Powell knew Walter had been captured by the Confederates. Someone reported seeing him raving mad at a prisoner-of-war camp.

And how could Major Powell earn a living for Emma and himself with only one arm?

3 Going West

Walter Powell came home from a Confederate prisoner-of-war camp forever changed. Before the war, he was a bright teacher. Now he stayed in dark, angry moods. For some reason, once in a while, he'd sing. No one knew why.

Major Powell's problem was the loss of his right hand. Determined to keep his independence, he practiced doing everyday tasks with his left. In time, he wrote letters, buttoned his shirts, mounted horses, and did all the other things he had to do to be on his own. If only the reddened stump on his right arm would stop hurting. The pain was impossible to ignore.

In 1865, Major Powell and Emma went back to Michigan and Illinois where their parents lived. Joseph had a suggestion for his son's occupation. Why not return to teaching? He didn't need two hands to teach. Despite their early differences, the Powell family was close. Major Powell listened. He wasn't one to hold grudges.

While Major Powell was in the army, he learned that he had received an honorary degree from Illinois Wesleyan University in Bloomington. No doubt this degree came from Joseph's connections at the university. The degree gave the college dropout the opportunity to become a professor of science at Wesleyan. Delighted, Major Powell was a tornado of energy and ideas. He put together a new science curriculum for the students. And he set up a small museum.

Once the museum was started, Major Powell was itchy to do something else. He changed universities and took a teaching and curator position at Illinois State Normal University, also located in Bloomington. The faculty knew Major Powell well. During the war, he'd sent them boxes of **invertebrate shells**, such as mollusks. Powell had collected many of the fifteen thousand shells in the collection at Illinois State Normal University.

In March 1867, this spirited professor had another thought. Why not take a collecting expedition to the territory of Colorado? Go see western nature specimens, soaring mountains, Native Americans, fast rivers, and colorful canyons. He'd take relatives, friends, students, and Emma with him. They'd help him collect specimens for the university.

Illinois State Normal University gave him $500 for the expedition, but it wasn't enough money. So he begged additional money and supplies from other universities and from his old commander, General Grant. Grant was now head of the Armies of the United States.

Twelve **greenhorns** left the summer of 1867 for Colorado Territory. Most had little experience as explorers or scientists, but greenhorns were all Powell could afford to pay. Never mind if they didn't have the scientific training; Professor Powell would instruct them on the way. Each member of the team assumed a particular job. They were listed as **ornithologists, zoologists, entomologists, herpetologists,** and **mineralogists.**

Everything was set. Emma—the only woman and an assistant ornithologist—and Major Powell left ahead of the others by train in late May 1867 to buy supplies for the **expedition.** The others followed the Powells and met them in Council Bluffs, Iowa. That's as far as the railroad had been built.

From there, the unprotected travelers followed each other in a wagon train along the Platte River to Denver,

Colorado Territory. Stagecoach stations, military posts, general stores, and blacksmith shops dotted the trail. But mostly the trail stretched across open prairie. The Powell expedition was nervous. There were reports of surprise Native American attacks on white settlers. The Native Americans were on the warpath because their hunting lands were being invaded.

Along the way, the travelers saw a wagon wheel smeared with blood and hair. Beside the wheel was a grave. If that wasn't enough to scare them, there were terrifying summer storms. Lightning crisscrossed the sky, followed by deafening thunder. And...those strong winds. Who knew when they might blow over a wagon?

On June 17, they came to Fort McPherson, Kansas. Two Civil War generals, William T. Sherman and George A. Custer, were there, too. The generals were in pursuit of the Native Americans. These conflicts between the Native Americans and the U.S. Army became known as the Indian Wars.

Rushing as fast as they could, the Powell expedition made it from Council Bluffs to Denver in forty days.

Denver was a rough frontier town in 1867. It had grown during the gold rush of 1859 to 40,000 residents, but now there were fewer than 5,000 along its dirt streets.

Denver was expensive. The Powell party soon left, heading south. Emma rode sidesaddle on a Mexican pony. They were on their way to climb glorious Pikes Peak in the Rocky Mountains.

On July 27, they began to climb. Even then, Pikes Peak was a tourist attraction. Many men had been there, but Emma was either the second or third white woman to climb to the top.

From Pikes Peak, they went west to South Park. Here they climbed Mount Lincoln. Now their wagons were full of specimens for the university museum. Powell, Emma, and the men had collected wildflowers, insects, dead animals, snakes, and birds. At Central City, they added mineral and **ore** samples.

Then it was back to Denver, where Major Powell gave a science lecture to tell what he knew about Colorado's natural history. He told of Colorado's long-ago sea and described tropical plants and animals now extinct. He told of decayed forests turning into coal. He explained that as the seas dried up over thousands of years, crevices formed that sometimes held gold.

In time, rain and frost broke up the rocks in the crevices and washed gold down to lower ground. Here it was dug out of the ground or panned from mountain streams by miners.

In September, the others returned to Illinois, but Major Powell and Emma stayed in Colorado for two more months. They went to Middle Park, North Park, and Grand Lake. An exciting new idea was forming in Major Powell's mind.

4 Gathering a Crew

One word written across maps of the West caught John Wesley Powell's attention. That word was *unexplored.* The unexplored areas of wilderness were in parts of southern Utah and northern Arizona. The area was two hundred miles north to south and three hundred miles east to west. It included what we know today as Colorado River's Grand Canyon. Powell wanted to be the first to do a thorough job of exploring and mapping this wilderness. That was his exciting plan.

There were two good reasons other explorers had not mapped this wilderness. One was danger. Even brave Native Americans refused to paddle the Colorado River through the Grand Canyon. Their knee-knocking stories told of the river disappearing underground and no one ever coming out. The second reason was that the

arid, rocky land was considered worthless. White settlers wanted to go where they could claim land and become farmers.

Before deciding his route through the unmapped areas, Major Powell needed to learn all he could about the Grand, Colorado, and Green rivers. He had to decide where to start the expedition and where it should end. So he headed back to Colorado in June 1868.

This time, he traveled further into the wilderness northwest of Denver. Emma and nineteen eager greenhorns came along. The greenhorns on this trip were students, ministers, his moody brother Walter, and Emma. Some knew something about science. Others didn't. Major Powell needed many workers to collect, identify, and pack up specimens. Sixty-seven colleges and schools helped pay for the expedition in exchange for the specimens Powell collected.

The group stepped off the train at Cheyenne, Wyoming. The first order of business was to buy horses. None could be found. Then **drovers** came to Cheyenne with a herd of bucking Mexican ponies that had never felt a saddle on their backs. Desperate, Major Powell bought them. After the horses stopped running away and were broken in enough to ride, the expedition headed south to Colorado.

Soon they disappeared into Colorado's vast back-country. They pushed through aspen groves, sagebrush, scrub oak, and pines to climb mountains and study rivers. This beautiful area was so remote that one member of the expedition was lost for over thirty days and, while he was missing, never saw another human being.

Major Powell climbed at least ten of Colorado's high peaks. His group made the first recorded climb to the top of Longs Peak. He also named one of the mountains, Mount Powell, after himself. Mount Powell is 13,560 feet high and is located in Eagles Nest Wilderness Area northeast of Vail, Colorado.

Major Powell climbed Longs Peak in the Colorado Rocky Mountains in 1868. Elevation at the summit is 14,251 feet.

Climbing these peaks was important. From the mountaintops, Powell could see possible overland routes and the courses of rivers.

After a summer of collecting and climbing, Powell split up the expedition. He led the larger group to Green River City, Wyoming. From there, they returned to Illinois. However, some of the expedition remained to winter in Powell Park, near present-day Meeker, Colorado. Among them were Emma and Walter.

That winter, Major Powell hustled to make preparations for the May 1869 exploration. There was much to be done.

The starting point would be Green River City, Wyoming. The recent arrival of the railroad to that small settlement gave Powell a place to gather supplies. The plan was to row south on the Green River to where it joined the Grand River (later renamed the Colorado River) and flowed together to become the Colorado River. Then they would head west on the Colorado River and on through what was later named the Grand Canyon.

Money to pay for the 1869 expedition came from many places. Free food—beans, coffee, bacon, flour, sugar, and dried apples—came from the army. To supplement this scanty diet, the crew would catch fish and shoot game. The Smithsonian Institution and the Chicago Academy of Science gave Major Powell scientific equipment. Now he had the necessary **thermometers, chronometers, barometers, sextants,** and **compasses.**

A sextant is used to calculate longitude and latitude. Major Powell had to know longitude and latitude to make accurate maps of the unexplored Grand Canyon.

Powell ordered and paid for four boats. That money came from the Illinois Natural History Society and the Illinois Industrial University. And, Powell and his wife put their own money into paying for the expedition.

They also brought ammunition for shooting game and tools for building and repairs. Because there was a possibility of staying over the winter, they brought extra clothes.

No one knew how long the exploration would take, so Major Powell took enough supplies for ten months.

The men Major Powell hired were as different from each other as coal is from gold.

Jack Sumner was a grumpy, capable hunter. He boasted that he had killed three grizzlies and two mountain lions and had crossed the Rocky Mountains in the middle of winter on snowshoes. He wasn't afraid of danger. After serving in the Civil War, he was a mountain guide and hunter. He'd be in charge when Powell was away from the expedition. The Howland brothers—Oramel and Seneca—were from Vermont. Oramel had worked as a printer and an editor at the *Rocky Mountain News.* Seneca was a quiet man, well liked. Billy Hawkins was the cook. Andy Hall, a jolly nineteen-year-old, had been a scout, a mule driver, and a boatman. Cool-headed and careful, George Bradley was a wounded Civil War veteran. Then there was the unwashed Bill Dunn, who stayed as far away as he could from soap and water. He'd been a trapper.

Know More!

In 1869 Powell had to choose which river—the Green or the Grand—he would travel to get to the Colorado River. He wisely chose the Green River as it is four hundred miles longer and is consistently deeper. In 1921, the state of Colorado, with help from the U.S. Congress, unfairly changed the Grand River's name to the Colorado. Because of its length and amount of water, the Green River should have received the honor of being renamed the Colorado.

‹◆›

*John C. (Jack) Sumner was one of the men who signed up
for the trip through the Grand Canyon.*

Frank Goodman, an Englishman, joined at the last
minute. He was so enthusiastic about going that he
offered to pay for his trip. Major Powell and his brother
Walter made up the rest of the party of ten.

They were tough, independent-minded, muscular men, filled with a sense of adventure. Most were mountain men and Civil War veterans, able to take care of themselves. The "gentlemen scientists" of the 1867 and 1868 expeditions had gone home to Illinois.

Four sturdy boats were shipped by train from Chicago to Green River City. They were built according to Major Powell's sketches. Three were twenty-one feet long, made of rugged oak, with watertight compartments on both ends. The fourth—the *Emma Dean*—was sixteen feet long, made of pine, and built to be fast.

Crew assignments were made. Sumner and Dunn were in the *Emma Dean* with Powell. Walter Powell and Bradley had responsibility for *Kitty Clyde's Sister.* The Howland brothers and Goodman manned the *No Name.* Hawkins and Hall rowed the *Maid of the Canyon.*

The boats were to follow each other in an orderly fashion. The *Emma Dean* first, then *Kitty Clyde's Sister, No Name,* and *Maid of the Canyon.* The Colorado River Exploring Expedition was ready to begin its voyage into the menacing rivers.

Meanwhile, Emma returned to her family in Detroit to wait and wonder.

❮◆❯

1. **Mount Morris,
   New York**
2. **Jackson, Ohio**
3. **South Grove, Wisconsin**
4. **St. Paul, Minnesota
   to New Orleans, Louisiana**
5. **Chicago, Illinois**
6. **Detroit, Michigan**
7. **Shiloh, Tennessee**
8. **Denver, Colorado**
9. **Green River City, Wyoming**
10. **Grand Canyon,
    Arizona**
11. **Washington, D.C.**
12. **Hopi Villages in the
    ancient province of Tusayan**
13. **Brooklin, Maine**

Important Places in
John Wesley Powell's Life

5 Dangerous Rivers

At one o'clock on the afternoon of May 24, 1869, the four boats and crew of the Colorado River Exploring Expedition pushed off from the shores of Green River City, Wyoming. They were on their way to explore and map the dangerous Green and Colorado rivers. The local folks stood onshore and cheered. An American flag waved on Major Powell's lead boat, the *Emma Dean*. The current quickly took the boats down the river, and they disappeared from sight.

Once on their way, Powell taught his crew flag signals. If there wasn't a safe passage around rocks and over waterfalls, he used flags to direct the boats behind him. A signal flag dipped to the left meant head to the left shore. One dipped to the right meant go to the right shore.

◀ ◆ ▶

When they approached rough areas of the rivers, Powell had two choices. He could attach lines to the boats and ease them through the rough waters. This was called **lining**. Or he could order the men to **portage**. That meant the men had to unload the supplies and carry them to calmer waters. Then they would have to hoist the four heavy boats on their shoulders and carry them. When they had carried everything past the dangerous waters, they reloaded the boats and continued on. Needless to say, the crew far preferred lining to portaging.

The start from Green River Station.

Major Powell in December 1869, a few months
after his first expedition through the Grand Canyon.

At first, the crew rowed awkwardly and got stuck on sandbars. That was to be expected. For the most part, these mountain men were amateurs on the river. But once they caught on, they found it great fun charging through high-spraying water around rocks and over small waterfalls. Soon they became expert boatmen.

Along the rivers, Major Powell often stopped to map the area and take scientific readings. He registered temperatures, measured altitudes, checked the time, and used compasses and sextants to draw maps. Members of the crew helped.

The compasses told Major Powell if they were traveling north, south, east, or west. The sextants showed their position on the earth's surface. Using a barometer, Major Powell measured the heights of cliffs and mountains. He also measured how many feet the party had to descend before reaching the end of the Grand Canyon. This was sobering news because it was thousands of feet. That meant the men had to row, line, or portage down many steep rocky rapids and waterfalls.

Jaw-dropping beauty followed them along the rivers. Heads turned to see colorful formations in shades of red, orange, purple, blue, yellow, green, white, black, and chocolate brown. On the tops and sides of these spectacular formations were cliffs, **pinnacles,** arches, towers, **buttes**, caves, and **minarets.**

Along the way, the expedition named many sites. There was Flaming Gorge, a beautiful area of red-orange stone that glowed in the setting sun. Andy Hall named a canyon Lodore after a poem he once read by Robert Southey, titled "The Cataract of Lodore." Then

1869 Colorado River Exploring Expedition

1. **May 24. Depart from Green River City, Wyoming**
2. **May 30. Flaming Gorge**
3. **June 9. Lodore Canyon, *No Name* crashes**
4. **June 16. Fire**
5. **June 18. Bradley rescues Powell**
6. **July 5. Goodman leaves**
7. **July 15. Bowknot Bend**
8. **July 17. The Green River and the Grand River join and become the Colorado River**
9. **July 26. Powell collects pitch to repair boats**
10. **July 29. Discover Native American village ruins**
11. **August 1. Walter sang *Old Shadey* in Glen Canyon**
12. **August 9. Marble Canyon**
13. **August 13. Enter the Grand Canyon**
14. **August 15. Bright Angel Creek**
15. **August 28. Howlands and Dunn leave**
16. **August 29. Float out of the Grand Canyon**

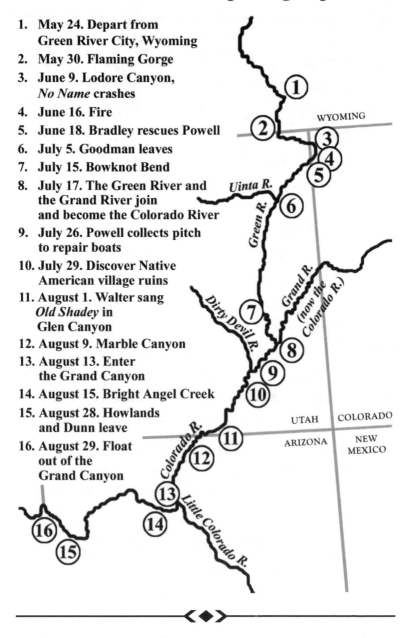

there was Bowknot Bend; Dirty Devil River, named for its bad smell; and Glen Canyon, where Walter Powell stood in a cavern and broke into song. Other places they named were a limestone-faced canyon they called Marble Canyon and Bright Angel Creek.

When they stopped, Major Powell wrote in his journals. Conquering his fear of heights, he sometimes perched on a ledge 2,000 feet above the river, legs dangling in space. He wrote of glorious scenery, amazing adventures, and a superb crew.

The crew members wrote, too. Sometimes, they presented a different story. They wrote their many complaints. They griped about rancid bacon, gagging on greasy beaver soup, and sifting sour lumps from their dwindling supply of flour. Slap! Pesky mosquitoes buzzed around their heads. Ouch! Bradley's shoes were gone, and he walked barefoot on brutally hot rocks. They were often drenched by rains, burned by the sun in temperatures that reached 116 degrees, and dunked in ice cold river water. They shivered at night in the cold air because most of the blankets had been lost in the river. And the lining and portaging were exhausting. Who could blame them for complaining?

Major Powell was constantly on the alert for hazards. He tried not to take any chances. In this wilderness, there was no one to help. They were on their own.

Even though Major Powell was careful, accidents happened. Early on, the Howland brothers and Goodman in the *No Name* didn't see a flag signal of danger ahead. They were in a fierce rapid, furiously bailing water out of the boat, when they whipped past Major Powell at breakneck speed. Suddenly, the *No Name* plunged over a small waterfall, then a huge one. Crash! Out of control, they hit one rock, then another. The *No Name* broke in two, spilling the crew and supplies into the churning water. Frank Goodman clung to a rock. The Howland brothers swam to an island. Jack Sumner leapt into the *Emma Dean*, rowed hard, and rescued the men.

It was a bitter lesson. Nearly one-third of their food supply had been swept away into the river. They also lost rifles, maps made, and notes written. Now the Howlands and Goodman had only the clothes they wore on their backs.

From then on, Major Powell ordered more of the dreaded linings and portages. He was nervous about boat wrecks.

More accidents came. One night, a wind blew the campfire sparks onto the grass. Whoosh! Their campground was in flames. Major Powell watched in horror

The fire in the camp.

from a cliff. He saw the crew run for the river. Bradley's neckerchief was on fire. Hawkins' clothes were on fire as he carried the mess kit, running for his life. Hawkins ran toward the boat, stumbled, and lost the mess kit in the river. When they came back to the scene, all they found were a few items from the mess kit—tin cups, basins, and a camp kettle.

All of this was too much for Goodman. He walked away from the camp into the wilderness and never came back.

Climbing with only one arm had its dangers too. Twice Major Powell was caught on ledges where he could not go up or down, left or right. The first time, Bradley was above him. Cool-headed in emergencies,

Bradley came up with a plan. He didn't have a rope, so he did the next best thing. He took off his pants and lowered them down to Powell. Major Powell let go of a rock with his only hand, quickly grabbed the pants, and Bradley hauled him off the narrow ledge.

The second time, Powell was stuck on a ledge 400 feet above the river. He yelled for help. Help came. The men climbed up, carrying boat oars. When they were close enough to him, they pressed the oars against Powell's body until he could inch his way to safety.

Bradley's quick thinking saved Major Powell's life.

Walter was a hero, too. At a bad rapid, he used powerful strokes to stay away from a harmful rock overhang.

Smack! A great wave hit the boat. Bradley was in grave danger. He was caught half in and half out of the boat. His foot was jammed inside the boat. His head was dragging under the water. Walter used all his strength to row away from the overhang, then reached over, grabbed Bradley, and yanked him back into the boat.

As they traveled the rivers, Major Powell often stopped to climb. He scrambled up and down the towering monuments and cliffs, carrying his measuring instruments. He collected artifacts and specimens. He studied the area's geology in the layers of rock. Sometimes he found the ruins of Native American villages and wondered who had lived there and why the villages were abandoned. He looked for wood to saw into new oars and pine **resin** to repair holes in the boats. To carry the resin back to the boats, he cut off his empty sleeve to make a little sack and carried a gallon of the resin down to smear on the boats.

As they entered the Grand Canyon and neared the end of their journey, the crew became short-tempered about Powell's delays. Their food was almost gone. So was their patience. They couldn't understand why Major Powell took precious time to explore and collect specimens. They wanted to keep going down the canyon and be done with the expedition.

Know More!

When Powell made the 1869 exploration, some called the Grand Canyon by another name. They called it Big Canyon. John Wesley Powell made the decision for the canyon's name. He instructed that the word "Grand" be written on topographical maps. That was it. From then on, it was called the Grand Canyon.

Then they came to the toughest section of the Grand Canyon. The hardest of rocks—jagged granite—clogged the rapids. Soaring cliffs of up to 3,000 feet surrounded them. Daylight was only a sliver of light more than a mile above them. Often the cliff walls were so close there was no shore where they could portage. Swift water nosed its way around huge rocks, sending high sprays of mist into the air, making it difficult to see.

The only food left was some musty flour, a few dried apples, and coffee.

One granite rapid followed another.

Major Powell stood on the boat, strapped to the **gunwales**, watching for safe passages through the rocks.

After months of experience, they were excellent rowers, but could they make it through this?

It was too much. The Howland brothers and Dunn quit. They begged Major Powell and the others to do the same. They were going to climb out of the canyon to safety—or so they thought.

Major Powell didn't know what to do. He couldn't continue on alone, not with just one hand. He paced all night. Then he woke the rest to ask whether the men would finish the journey. They said they would. Hawkins remembered that Major Powell put his arm around him, tears running down his cheeks.

In the morning, Major Powell graciously offered to share the little remaining food with the Howlands and Dunn. The three politely refused and said they would find some at the top. Nevertheless, Hawkins put some biscuits on a rock and hoped they'd take them. The three men were given two rifles and a shotgun. It was a sad farewell.

Down to only six men, the remaining crew left the *Emma Dean* behind in case the Howlands and Dunn had second thoughts.

Then they got into the battered *Maid of the Canyon* and *Kitty Clyde's Sister*. They pulled hard on the oars through more whirlpools, great waves, and waters that had been whipped into white foam.

Again, they tried to line the boats.

Everyone was onshore except Bradley. He was in the *Maid of the Canyon*, using an oar to push the boat away from a rocky cliff. The men onshore tied a line to the boat and began to ease it forward. But they ran out of rope at the edge of a waterfall. The *Maid of the Canyon* began to slam against the cliff. What to do? They tied their line around a rock and rushed back to get more line out of *Kitty Clyde's Sister.* As they did, the *Maid of the Canyon* crashed again and again against the cliff. Rather than let the boat break, Bradley cut the line. The boat plunged over the waterfall and disappeared from sight in white foam. Suddenly, Bradley popped into view, waving his hat. But Powell wondered if Bradley was safe in the damaged *Maid of the Canyon.* Major Powell and Sumner jumped into the *Kitty Clyde's Sister.* Away they went, shooting over the falls. Their boat filled with water, rolled over, and tossed them out. But they were lucky. Bradley snatched them from the river.

That was the last frightening incident. The expedition into the unmapped waters of the Green and Colorado rivers was a success.

On August 29, they floated out of the canyon. That night by a campfire, they celebrated and talked of their adventures. Major Powell wrote in *The Exploration of the Colorado River and Its Canyons,* "Now the danger is over, now the toil has ceased, now the gloom has disappeared,...The river rolls by us in silent majesty; the quiet of the campground is sweet; our joy is almost ecstasy. We sit till long after midnight talking of the Grand Canyon, talking of home, but talking chiefly of the three men who left us."

The Grand Canyon

On August 30, 1869, they met three Mormon settlers and one Native American. The Mormons were surprised to see any of the expedition alive. They had been asked to look for debris. News quickly spread to the Mormon community that the Colorado River Exploring Expedition had arrived. A Mormon bishop hurried to them with a wagonload of fresh melons and mail from home.

The expedition had taken 69 days and covered over 900 miles.

But where were the Howlands and Dunn?

No one knew.

6 Hopi Villages

After John Wesley Powell's famous 1869 expedition through the Grand Canyon, he came back to survey the West many times. As he surveyed, he collected information and artifacts from Native Americans who called the West home.

Major Powell knew their way of life was quickly disappearing. White settlers were claiming the land, and Native American tribes were being sent to reservations. There were many tribes, and these tribes were different from each other in language, dress, and culture. Without written languages, Powell knew their histories would soon be lost.

Powell had long been fascinated by Native Americans. As a boy, he collected arrowheads and other artifacts for George Crookham's museum. As a teenager, he felt sympathy for the ragged and hungry

Terraced homes in Oraibi village were built of stone and mortar and were three or four stories high. They were built facing east on a mesa 200 feet above the plains below.

Winnebagoes who rested beside a creek on the Powell's Wisconsin farm. Later, while exploring Colorado, he visited the Utes. Then on the famous 1869 expedition, high on cliffs above the Colorado River, he saw the abandoned villages.

Now Powell was back in the West. He had not for-
gotten those village ruins. He had heard that Hopi
lived in similar villages in northern Arizona. He decided to take a small expedition to find them. He wrote
about meeting the Hopi in an article entitled, *The
Ancient Province of Tusayan.*

Two Native American guides and others—one a
Mormon named Hamblin—came to help. The guides
names were Na-pu (Old Man) and To-ko-puts (Wild
Cat). Their job would be to locate water holes, as well
as the Hopi people.

As they rode on horseback through unknown territory, Major Powell noticed Na-pu was unhappy. He wondered why, so he asked the old man what was wrong. Indignantly, Na-pu said that it was he who told To-ko-puts where the water holes were, but To-ko-puts ran ahead, lit a smoke signal at the hole, and got all the credit from Powell's men for finding it. Powell understood. Na-pu's feelings were hurt. He comforted Na-pu by telling him that the two of them were the wise elders of the expedition. Na-pu liked what he heard. From then on, he stayed close to Powell.

Na-pu and To-ko-puts found the water holes, but the location of the Tusayan villages was a riddle. So they asked strangers from other tribes for directions. The problem was that the tribes didn't understand each other's spoken languages. So how could they communicate?

Major Powell tells us how.

He said that Native Americans had many ways to communicate. These smart people didn't rely only on spoken words. They also used facial and body expressions, drawings, and even their fingers and toes.

Powell wrote, "Whenever an Indian's tongue is tied, he can talk all over; and so they make gestures, struck attitudes, grunted, frowned, laughed, and altogether had a lively time."

Drawings were forms of communication, too. Once, when Powell's guides needed directions, a Native American stranger knelt in the sand and used his finger to draw a map.

To communicate numbers, the Native Americans used fingers and toes. When Major Powell asked four men how many people were in their tribe, the men sat down on the ground. They divided the village families among them.

Then each man counted his allotted families on his fingers and toes. Afterward, the Native Americans

gathered sticks, one for each tribal member. They gave the sticks to Powell, and he counted them. There were seventy-three people in the tribe.

After making their way up and down steep, rocky cliffs and canyons, the expedition found the Hopi. They lived in seven villages named Oraibi, Shi-pau-i-luv-i, Mi-shong-i-ni-vi, Shong-a-pa-vi, Te-wa, Wol-pi, and Si-choam-a-vi. Altogether, there were about 2,700 people.

The Hopi lived on mesa tops in houses stacked one on top of the other. Ladders connected the different levels. Little children, nimble as young mountain sheep, ran up and down these ladders from one floor to the other.

The Hopi were polite, hospitable people. Major Powell wrote, "Enter a house and you are invited to take a seat on a mat placed for you upon the floor, and some refreshment is offered—perhaps a melon with a little bread, perhaps peaches or apricots. After you have eaten, everything is carefully cleaned away, and, with a little broom made of feathers, the matron or her daughter removes any crumbs or seeds which may have been dropped."

The Hopi men dressed in moccasins, leggings, shirts, and blankets. The women wore high-topped

moccasins, short pet-
ticoats dyed black
that sometimes had a
red border around
the bottom, a shawl,
and a girdle of many
colors around their
waists.

The women's
long, black, shiny
hair required great

Unmarried Hopi women wore their hair in flat coils covering their ears.

care. The women washed their hair in soap made from
the root of the **yucca** plant. Married women wore
their hair braided and rolled into a knot at the back of
their heads. Unmarried women parted their hair in the
middle, braided each side, then rolled the braids into
coils that covered each ear.

Major Powell wrote of their daily schedule. "At
dawn of day the governor of the town goes up to the
top of his house and calls on the people to come forth.
In a few moments the upper story of the town is covered with men, women, and children. For a few minutes he **harangues** them on the duties of the day."

After this the people prayed, exercised, ate their
breakfast, and went to work in the fields tending their

crops or to the kiva. The kiva was an underground room used for religious ceremonies or as a place to gather to visit.

Powell visited other tribes. It was the friendly Shivwit tribe who gave Powell an answer to the mysterious disappearance of the Howland brothers and Dunn. The Shivwits offered an apology. They confessed they had killed the men. It was a mistake. The Shivwits had been lied to. They were told by other Native Americans that the three men had viciously murdered a Hualapai woman. With that apology, Powell ended his inquiry. He had his answer to the mystery of what had happened to the men.

TUSAYAN TRAY:
Piki, *or bread, and other foods were served on beautiful trays like this one. To make piki, corn was separated by color and ground to make a thick gruel. The gruel was smeared on top of a hot stone to bake in a thin layer. The layers of bread could be white, yellow, red, blue, or black, depending on the type of corn used.*

In 1872, Major Powell, Emma, and their little daughter, Mary, moved to Washington, D.C. They bought a three-story townhouse at 910 M Street, N.W.

At the nation's capital, Powell established the Bureau of Ethnology in the Smithsonian Institution in 1879. His star was rising. He was considered an authority on the West. People listened to what he had to say. Powell now had a department that could concentrate on collecting information about Native Americans.

To Powell, the Native Americans were never "savages" as they were called by some who lived at that time. They had the same intelligence as the whites, but they did not have the same knowledge about science. Powell respected their uniqueness. He wanted to save as much information as he could about the tribes' different religions, languages, and ways of doing things.

Powell needed a staff to help him acquire the information. Eyebrows raised when people saw Powell hire women as well as men. That was unheard of in the 1800s when few women worked outside of their homes. That didn't bother Major Powell. He hired them anyway.

One of his staff's amazing accomplishments was to

identify five hundred different Native American languages. Powell knew this was only the beginning. He said that when Columbus came to America, several thousand languages were spoken.

Powell is remembered for his work with the Native Americans. He also is remembered for his other mission. Today, that mission brings fresh fruits and vegetables to our dinner table.

7 Honors

During the years that John Wesley Powell was the first director of the U.S. Bureau of Ethnology in Washington, D.C., he also became the second director of the U.S. Geological Survey. Powell was an excellent organizer. He could manage two departments successfully at the same time. The Geological Survey and its responsibility of water management became another of Powell's missions.

The Geological Survey had the job of creating **topographical** maps by surveying the United States. These maps showed the beginnings (sources) of our rivers and the wide variety of lands—mountains, plains, deserts—they flowed through. And it showed where the rivers ended (mouth). From the maps, Major Powell could see the big picture of how much water was available to the people of the United States and where it was located.

He knew water had to be managed. He had seen the Mormons and the Native Americans irrigating their growing crops. Without irrigation, they would have starved. These people built communities near rivers and springs. Then they built trenches to direct the water to their productive gardens. Powell thought the rest of America could learn to plan water use as the Mormons and Native Americans had. Engineers, using scientific methods, could plug the rivers with dams and direct their waters into **hydropower**, irrigation, and to meet other water needs.

All of this was in Major Powell's mind. It wasn't on the grand scale of dams and reservoirs we see today, but the ideas were starting. In time, these ideas became the foundation of the Bureau of Reclamation. This was the part of government that dealt with storing, sharing, and development of water for arid lands. Irrigation is why we can have fresh fruits and vegetables on our tables today.

While he headed two large government agencies, John Wesley Powell's influence grew. He was one of the first to recommend the Grand Canyon be made into a national park.

President James Garfield was Powell's close friend. Garfield insisted Powell write about his western experiences. Garfield told Powell that if he wanted government funds for scientific work, he had to write his exploration story.

He became a personal friend of President James Garfield and Alexander Graham Bell, the inventor of the telephone.

He either started or was a member of several clubs where bright scientific minds of the day came together. The clubs included the Anthropological Society, a biological society, a chemical society, and an entomological society. In 1888, Major Powell was one of thirty-three men who helped form the National Geographic Society.

To Powell's credit, and although he was a powerful figure in government, he was never involved in any political scandal.

For his lifetime accomplishments, John Wesley Powell received several honorary degrees. Honorary degrees are special awards given to people who made significant contributions to society but are not graduates of the university or college granting the degree. Harvard bestowed a doctor of laws. Important dignitaries were at the ceremony, including President

Grover Cleveland. Illinois Wesleyan gave him a master's degree and a doctorate. Columbian University—later named George Washington University—made him doctor of laws. And Heidelberg, a European university, gave him a doctorate. These were moments of glory for this self-taught, gutsy patriot who never finished college.

Perhaps the greatest tribute to him was naming a Colorado River reservoir Lake Powell, after him. Built in 1963, Lake Powell covers Glen Canyon, where Walter Powell sang so long ago.

In his last years, Major Powell spent his summers in a cottage in Brooklin, Maine. Here by the ocean, he enjoyed a simpler life of visiting with old friends, reading, and writing. Alexander Graham Bell regularly visited Powell on his way home to Nova Scotia.

Then, in January 1902, Major Powell had a cerebral hemorrhage. That fine mind and body he had on his expeditions was forever gone. He died on Tuesday, September 23, 1902.

Emma and daughter Mary brought his body back to Washington, D.C. He was buried with full military honors at Arlington National Cemetery. A burial at Arlington was befitting for this American hero. For it was John Wesley Powell who explored what others thought was impossible to explore; respected and preserved Native American cultures; and had a vision for the wise use of America's waters so they would serve the needs of all its citizens, not just a few.

On John Wesley Powell's tombstone are the words, *Soldier. Explorer. Scientist.*

Epilogue

FAMILY MEMBERS

Mary and Joseph Powell – Mary and Joseph are buried beside each other in Wheaton, Illinois. In his old age and after Mary died, Joseph did go west. He took the train to Denver, then back to Kansas to live with his daughter, Lida. The Powells raised a close family who were well educated for their time. Several were teachers, Nellie helped to get women the right to vote, and Bramwell became a famous educational reformer.

Walter Powell – He was passed from one sister's care to another's until they could no longer care for him. He died in 1915 in an asylum.

Emma Powell – Little is known about Emma after the expeditions. In Washington, D.C., she entertained friends who came for tea and conversation. And she took care of their daughter, Mary. After Major Powell's death, she had little income. She died in 1924.

Mary Powell – A quiet, nervous girl, she lived at home with her parents. She never married or had a career. On Sunday, September 23, 1934, she attended a ceremony for a memorial to Major Powell in Jackson, Ohio.

EXPEDITION MEMBERS

Long after the 1869 expedition, Major Powell wrote, "Their bronzed, hardy, brave faces come before me as they appeared in the vigor of life; their lithe but powerful forms seem to move around me; and the memory of the men and their heroic deeds, the men and their generous acts, overwhelms me with a joy."

George Bradley – Had an orchard business in San Diego, California. He died in 1885.

Bill Dunn – Killed by Native Americans, along with the Howlands, after they left the expedition and climbed out of the Grand Canyon.

Frank Goodman – No one knows what happened to him.

Andy Hall – He became a stagecoach guard and was killed by robbers in 1882.

Billy Hawkins – No one knew his past, but it was suspected he had been in trouble with the law. He settled in Arizona and became a justice of the peace, where he died in 1919.

Oramel and Senca Howland – Killed by Native Americans after they left the expedition and climbed out of the Grand Canyon.

Walter Powell – After the expedition, he was cared for by his sisters. His mental health grew worse, and he died in 1915 in an asylum.

Jack Sumner – Sumner became a sour old man who barely scratched out a living mining in Utah. He thought of himself as the man who discovered the Grand Canyon. He died in 1907.

Timeline

March 24, 1834 – John Wesley Powell born at Mount Morris, New York.

1843 – Nine-year-old Wes lives with George Crookham.

1846 – Powell family moves to Walworth County, Wisconsin.

1850 – Wes leaves home to go to school in Janesville, Wisconsin.

1852 – Wes teaches school in Jefferson County, Wisconsin.

1855 – Walks from St. Paul, Minnesota to Detroit, Michigan. Meets his future wife, Emma Dean.

1856 – Rows boat from St. Paul, Minnesota to New Orleans, Louisiana.

1861 – Joins Union Army and marries Emma.

1862 – Wounded in the Battle of Shiloh. Arm amputated.

1865 – Begins teaching at Illinois Wesleyan University.

‹◆›

1867 – Leads first expedition to Colorado.

1868 – Second expedition to Colorado.

May 24, 1869 – Colorado River Exploring Expedition begins at Green River City, Wyoming.

August 29, 1869 – Expedition ends after leaving Grand Canyon.

1879 – Establishes the U. S. Bureau of Ethnology.

1881 – Heads the United States Geological Survey.

September 23, 1902 – John Wesley Powell dies.

Glossary

archaeology – science that studies the history and culture of ancient people

arid – dry; an area with very little rainfall

artifacts – objects made by human hands, such as a tool or piece of pottery

artillery – a branch of the military that is armed with large firearms such as cannons

barometers – instruments used to measure atmospheric pressure

biology – the study of living things

buttes – steep hills standing alone on a plain

chemistry – the science that deals with the composition, structure, and properties of substances

chronometers – instruments that measure time

compasses – instruments that show directions such as north, south, east, and west

curator – person in charge of a place of exhibits, such as a museum

drovers – people who herd animals to market

emigrate – to leave one's country

entomologists – scientists who study insects

ethnology – the science that compares human cultures

expedition – a journey

fossils – remains or traces of plant or animal life that have been left in rock

geography – science that studies the surface of the earth

geology – science that studies the physical nature and history of the earth

greenhorns – inexperienced people

gunwales – upper edges on the sides of a boat

harangues – to give noisy speeches

herpetologists – scientists who study reptiles and amphibians

hydropower – power produced by using water, such as by a waterwheel

immigrants – people who come to a new country

invertebrate shells – covering for an animal without a backbone, such as a clam

lining – easing a boat through dangerous waters by tying and pulling from the shore

mineralogists – scientists who study rocks and other non-living substances from the earth

minarets – tall, slender towers

mollusk – invertebrate animal such as a clam or snail

natural history – study of plants, animals, minerals, and geology

natural history museum – a museum that displays artifacts and specimens from nature

ore – a mineral that contains a valuable metal for which it is mined

ornithologists – scientists who study birds

pinnacles – the highest peaks

portage – carrying boats and their contents overland

resin – the sticky sap of pine trees

sextants – instruments to calculate longitude and latitude

specimen – a part of a whole. An example is a rock from a cliff

surveying – determining the location, form, or boundaries of an area by measuring the lines and angles in using geometry and trigonometry

topographical map – a map that shows the details of the earth's surface, such as mountains, rivers, and plains

tourniquet – a device that stops bleeding

underground railroad – neither underground nor a railroad, but a system of people who helped slaves escape to the North prior to the Civil War

vandals – people who purposely destroy or damage another's property

yucca – a plant with stiff, sword-shaped leaves and white flowers

zoologists – scientists who study animals

Bibliography

Ervin, Robert. *Powell Memorial.* Jackson, Ohio, 2005.

Ervin, Robert. *John Wesley Powell.* Jackson, Ohio, 2005.

Fraser, Mary Ann. *In Search of the Grand Canyon.* New York: Henry Holt and Company, 1995.

Murphy, Dan. *John Wesley Powell, Voyage of Discovery: The Story Behind the Scenery.* Las Vegas, Nevada: KC Publications, Inc., 1991.

Powell, John Wesley. *The Exploration of the Colorado River and Its Canyons.* New York: Penquin Books, 1997 (1875).

Powell, Major J. W. *The Hopi Villages: The Ancient Province of Tusayan.* Palmer Lake, Colorado: Filter Press, 1972 (1875).

Rusho, W. L. *Powell's Canyon Voyage.* Palmer Lake, Colorado: Filter Press, 1969.

Terrell, John Upton. *The Man Who Rediscovered America.* New York: Weybright and Talley, Inc., 1969.

Worster, Donald. *A River Running West.* New York: Oxford University Press, Inc., 2001.

Index

How to Use a Compass
by Alan Cook

"Mom, Dickens and I are going for a boat ride," said Annalise, heading for the dock.

"Be careful," answered her mother.

Dickens raced ahead of Annalise, barking. He jumped on the boat, ran to the front, and placed his paws on the bow.

Annalise got out the life jackets, one for herself and another for Dickens. She checked the gas and oil, switched on the boat's running lights, and felt in her pocket for the cell phone and compass.

She shook her head. The compass was new. She didn't know how to use it. She decided to get instructions when she got home. Annalise started the engine and left the dock.

Annalise headed out at full throttle. She knew how to captain a boat. They skipped over the waves, turned in circles, and watched for other boaters.

‹◆›

Then Annalise frowned. A gray fog was moving toward them, coming in fast. Within minutes, she couldn't see where to go. Dickens got down from the bow, whimpered, and laid his head against her leg.

Annalise called her mother on the cell phone.

"Mom, I can't see and I don't know where to go," she said, her voice cracking.

"Annalise," said her mother, "look at the red tip of your compass. It always points to the top of the earth at magnetic north."

Annalise did as she was told.

"There are four points on your compass dial," continued her Mother. "Magnetic north is 0 degrees, east is 90 degrees, south is 180 degrees, and west is 270 degrees. When you left the dock, you were heading straight west so…"

"I go east to come back to the dock," said Annalise.

"Right," Mother answered. "Now turn the bow of the boat to line up with magnetic north."

Annalise did. She slowly turned the boat until her compass needle showed magnetic north.

"Now turn the bow east to 90 degrees and hold that course," said her mother. "I'll be on the dock listening for the motor."

Carefully, Annalise made her way back through the dense fog.

Suddenly, Dickens began to bark and wag his tail.

Annalise smiled.

She saw the dock and her mother.

Annalise tucked the compass into her pocket and tied the boat to the dock. She gave her mother a hug. Tomorrow I'll learn more, she thought, with a shiver. But for now, I'm just grateful the compass brought us safely home.

Acknowledgments

My thanks to all who graciously brought their expertise to this book. The students at Discovery Canyon Campus, their teacher Mary Beth Blake, and the library media specialist, Barbara Linnenbrink. They brought a fresh perspective and valuable direction to the story. Historian Bob Ervin and the Jackson Historical Society for their work on the life of John Wesley Powell. Artists Susan Blanton and David W. Jones. The Utah Historical Society, the National Archives, and the U.S. Geological Survey for photographs. Jill Jensen and Leona Lacroix for editing. Alan Cook for writing the story about compasses. And, to Doris Baker of Filter Press for her dedication to and excellence in biographical books for students of history.

About the Author

Jean Thor Cook and her husband, Alan, are passionate about history and travel. They visit historical museums in Mexico, Canada, Europe, and America. Among them have been several John Wesley Powell sites. Always, they are inspired by this patriot who risked his life and forever maimed his body for America. The author believes John Wesley Powell's life is a model for us today. It is a story she feels privileged to tell.

Other works by the author include: *Who's Under My Bed, Audrey and the Nighttime Skies, Sam the Terror of Westbrook Elementary, Butterflies for Grandpa, Hugs For Our New Baby, Room For A Stepdaddy, Los Amiguitos' Fiesta,* and *Jesus Calms the Storm.*

More
Now You Know Bios

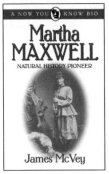
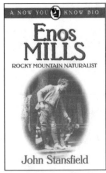
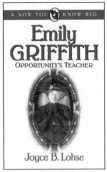